IMPROVING THE STATE

THE NATURAL ORDER

Tarl Warwick 2017

COPYRIGHT AND DISCLAIMER

INTRODUCTION

The concept of states has always been one of necessary difficulty; there are enough paradoxes, real and imagined, within the realm of society and politics, to make it seemingly untenable to even discuss the various forms of government and their improvement in accordance with some foundation dreamed up by any individual seeking to craft one; indeed, sometimes the worst forms of government have evolved out of primordial misunderstanding; we see no better example of this than communism, wherein Marx based a large proportion of his theory on the twofold concept he himself made from his office, without the benefit of modern archaeological discovery. His twofold basis was, of course, first, that man was communal when primitive (now a debunked notion) and second to this that because he had been communal in his archaic infancy, that communal forms of societal order were biologically innate and thus capable of both being used and used to good effect. That Marx was wrong is now clear; he was not alive to see the discovery of Gobekli Tepe push human order back by several thousand years, and in his time period human history was reckoned even to begin largely after Sumeria, no earlier than the time of the pyramids in Egypt. Perhaps he would have abandoned his theories altogether faced with this new knowledge. The road to Hell, here, was surely paved with good intentions, and the offshoots of his work proceeded to butcher perhaps a hundred million individuals over the following century. Not through malice but through ignorance, Marx stands as the single most murderous human being to ever exist, solely because of what others did in adapting his writings.

I am of the opinion that human systems which work, do so following an evolutionary basis. It is generally regarded as true that human language, human culture, architecture, and other human endeavors follow an evolutionary path (which depending on the level of artificial intervention are either closer to or further from natural versus artificial selection.) When I regard this, and I view the long span of human order, with its development in different and often reactionary directions over time, I can speculate only that a few things are true.

First, human governance is also subject to evolutionary processes. That which does not work is challenged, and should ot persist in its disarray it will fail.

Second, governance is not insular, nor is the state, but develops with, and often as the result of, technological advances (here we may observe the radical societal changes following in the wake of the first printing press, or the internet, or any similar paradigm-shifting development, especially in the realm of human communication.)

Third, evolutionary processes are not intelligently directed unless by human order itself, and then the direction to be used is the result of a second layer of competition; often between two or more governing bodies, nations, tribes, or ethnic groups. Sometimes, it is even the result of struggle between classes, races, or the population in part or whole against a tyrannical order (for example, the interplay between the governments of states held under wanton colonial power; the United States evolved from this chaos.)

Fourth, under such observations, we can determine simply what "works" and what does not, adopt it, make it semi-malleable, constrained in some ways but free flowing in others, to create a system resistant to extinction due to the two natural causes; tyranny (too much order) and anarchy (too little.)

IMPROVING THE STATE

Indeed these are the two methods by which states most often breathe their last gasp. Many otherwise adept, well ordered states fell into chaos and were subsumed from within or without because of a lack of good order. Many states fell to the same fate over time because their order was excessive. We might liken these two unfortunate conditions to diseases, after a sort; the nation is a body, a life form, an organism; it requires a brain to order it, but when that brain becomes obsessed with organization to a rabid degree it strangulates the organism in the same way which we may observe in a lunatic, whose obsessions, strange proclivities, and delusions eventually lead to its institutionalization or, often, suicide or other premature death. This lunatic is sometimes the usurpation of a free people by tyranny of one form or another, but often it is a slower process; a slow-growing cancer of the mind as bureaucracy replicates itself in a manner not unlike a tumor, no longer experiencing proper cellular controls to keep it from simply multiplying its own cells out of control and metastasizing.

How then does one stabilize a state? Even great empires fall into disunity through one of these two poles, between which is a combination, more or less, of good order and yet freedom and efficiency. For that is the interplay- you can maximize liberty and yet have tyranny regardless- a tyranny grown out of some non-state order; mob rule, anarchism, and so forth. You can also maximize order and yet it leads to a system which is either erratic and subject to autocratic and negative change, or abuse leading to revolution (and often anarchy anyways!) or an inefficient system as most are today, in which order begins to be shunned and seen as the subject of satire or derision by especially the literate but employed middle or working classes. This is the worst fate of all and evolves into a population that will begin to even abuse one another without regards to their actual abusers.

IMPROVING THE STATE

I will suggest here some general concepts which may be used to craft a better state. I am a civic nationalist- I am also a libertarian of sorts. To constrain government to certain roles is good, to allow it to instill the rudiments of order is also good. I will say here that libertarians (classical liberals) often are merely anarchists that I have little in common with; the concept of having no form of taxation and no genuine power structure is not even a full step from anarchy. I will also say here that some nationalists so-called in the modern age are not nationalists at all (they do not appear to notice the presence of 'nation' in their chosen title!) but rather tribalists of some sense that don't seem to understand that under the systems they propose, they're one autocrat's death from communism or any other abusive system, which can be instituted at a whim by whoever has the most guns backing them.

When I state here "perfecting" the state I do not mean crafting a utopia (we must be careful with such endeavors as we have seen over centuries of time) but rather creating a state based upon sound biological principles that is capable of functioning long term without breaking down. The very concept of senescence operates upon states regardless of how well ordered and proper they are and a population will inevitably have to deal with the eventual anarchic revolution or fascist takeover, war, epidemic, natural disasters, economic problems, and so forth, both natural and artificial. It remains then not to craft an eternal, stagnant state, but one capable of being malleable within acceptable confines, such that it is resistant to change when change is not needed, but open to it within a proper framework when it is necessary.

PERFECTING THE STATE

I: On Authoritarianism and Other Concepts

What must be said first before what can work is delineated is that which has been shown in various ways *not* to work. Here partly the argument must rely on the basis of the principles of biology; for the concept of the state and population and human endeavors being tied to and subjugated to evolution and biological overlap within this work is key. However, it is not necessary to delve into any complicated biological minutiae to describe the shortcomings of systems which have been attempted and which did not pan out (often repeatedly.)

First let me make an observation that common knowledge with regards to government is wrong in one simple but important way; we often hear the terms "fascism", "statism", "totalitarianism", "nazism" and so forth bandied around in a wanton manner, as though they meant the same thing and were just synonyms for the same basic concept. I reject this tendency and will make this far more simple. I can sum up the truth in one sentence:

We are all authoritarians, what remains is to determine the source of authority and its role and degree.

I imagine any libertarians or, indeed, civic nationalists reading this work just cocked their head and gave a sideways glance at anyone nearby as they grew confused so perhaps it is necessary to briefly explain how even an anarchist or libertarian is, still, an authoritarian.

Authoritarianism is invariably defined in a more proper

7

context as a centralized and often abusive system of government; but in common parlance it has become little more than a buzz word slapped onto any form of governance one does not like. Perhaps a more appropriate notion is that it is merely the di-pole to anarchic tendencies and the worship of order at large. Is not every form of governance and every societal system, no matter how decentralized, given then to this tendency?

The monarchist is an authoritarian who believes authority comes from a bloodline and is limitless.

The oligarchist is an authoritarian who believes it comes from a council or group of elites and is virtually limitless.

The statist is an authoritarian who believes it comes from a civic structure and is potentially limitless.

The communist (in pure form) is an authoritarian who believes it comes from collective will in a degraded and decentralized form and is limitless but somehow limited by people's primitive communal tendencies.

The libertarian (classical liberal) is an authoritarian who prefers the majority of authority be dispensed by an individual with the rudiments of a limited state.

The anarchist is an authoritarian who prefers all authority be dispensed by an individual in the absence of a state.

The ethnonationalist-fascist believes it comes from a combination civic and tribal state and is limitless on external matters but, perhaps, limited internally.

We come to an interesting concept here where a monarchy or oligarchy could, if constrained by a constitution and an armed population, technically function as a form of libertarian state. As far as I know this has not been achieved in the real world and is utopian and incapable of working, but it's an interesting idea on paper I suppose.

Here then we must discuss the matter of power itself; indeed it does corrupt. How then does a state or lack thereof compensate for it? In a monarchy, any benevolent king or queen may be followed by a tyrant. In an oligarchy the council may abuse at a whim and dissolve any constraint structure meant to prevent the same. Often, a government begins its abuse first by wooing the military that must in general exist of necessity because of the state of modern warfare.

In the anarchic state (and this is why anarchy first of all cannot actually function) all the population, empowered as it is, will degrade and corrupt itself and this inevitably becomes mob rule. This utopian concept is, in a pure state, short lived and miserable. We can simply observe the span of human history post-Marx and understand (generally) the failure of communism as well, which even its adherents sometimes claim has "never been tried"- indeed, the system is so totally antithetical to human nature that even its own proponents never use it and warp the social and political fabric of an upstart stateless Marxism movement into Stalinism, Maoism, or some other authoritarian variant thereupon.

Because different people even within ideologies hold different beliefs, it can be slightly difficult at times to even fully classify them without facing a tidal wave of "No True Scotsman" arguments. In the current age it is common enough for people to not understand their own stated principles that often they argue against tenets or substance from the same system they claim to support; a pro-state communist, a monarchist that claims blood lineage is unimportant, etc.

IMPROVING THE STATE

I am a proponent of nationalism myself; not nationalism in the sense of tribal identity, or even strictly civic nationalism, but rather libertarian nationalism. I identify the classical liberalism of the revolutionary period as the true posture of the United States and the exact ingrained spirit responsible for its very existence; the concept of a significantly constrained state, an armed population, and so forth. And this brings a second issue to the fore that must be briefly mentioned.

I base my understanding of mankind's states and societies on biology; I therefore have to admit for the existence of continued selective processes perturbing the direction of human evolution on a post-individualistic scale within society, language, and other human constructs. As such, it is important to admit that not all states were founded similarly. True, the United States grabbed its classical model from revolutionary France with some borrowing from ancient Rome and Greece, but Europe is comprised of states (more or less, due to malleable borders over time, especially post WWI and post cold war) which have been constructed by ethnic groups, and which functioned as ethnostates until very, very recently- indeed the social alienation of European culture by its own governments bringing in foreigners is far greater than any alienation we here faced during the waves of Irish, Chinese, or other immigrants here in the Americas. That is due to the state of our founding-Europe on the ethnostate principle (even before the concept existed) and the Americas on a civic foundation. What works for us cannot work for Europe, and what works for Europe cannot work for the Americas. What works for Asia will work for neither. And while there is interchange as evolution takes place and some nations adopt principles from others, grand overhauls of extant systems must be observed and, if more problems than solutions arise (take modern Europe's displacement level immigration from the islamic world for example) it should be stripped away and ended as quickly as possible.

II: Goals, and the Suffering of Modernity

Indeed the greatest goal is that the state should reflect simple biological reality. Like a human being is technically an amalgamation of highly differentiated primordial bacteria working in tandem to preserve their ability to replicate and maintain homeostasis, the state is comprised of individuals that nonetheless have pulled together to work for a similar common cause. If the state, for example, abuses the poor, it will inevitably face repercussions. If it should collapse its middle class, or attack the rich, or should it be poisoned by subversion and foreign ideologies which grind down its ability to function. When we observe immigration what we see is nothing more than the consumption and absorption of cellular units by one state from another in what amounts more often to the feeding of an animal on a corpse than direct predation on the living. Indeed, most states destroy themselves, and most people do the same; foreign hostility is almost never as terrifying in scope or action as directly internal action. For all of the wars of the Middle Ages, more peasant serfs died of famine or disease or abuse in their own lands than ever died in warfare itself.

For the subject of immigration we might liken the same to a biological system even further. We would not expect, for example, a carnivore to benefit from consuming more than tiny amounts of foliage, or an herbivore from consuming more than the occasional insect outside of its normal diet of photosynthetic life forms. Should any of these species consume too much of the wrong thing, it will become ill, and chronically so, perhaps, should it continue. States are not all the same- they have different values and different economic situations. A weak state must satiate itself with the right materials to improve its stature, and a strong state must avoid becoming weak. We have seen this sort of problem on both ends before.

11

IMPROVING THE STATE

Additionally the values of a state may be better or worse for any given situation in time as well. The enlightenment of France which brought about such great wealth of knowledge, such fine art and music, such grandiose and spectacular academia, did not serve it well when the era flipped over and conquest alone was on the minds of its competitors. As such, when war began in Europe, France suffered massively at the hands of cultures which had developed a more military-minded system. In eras of peace (which in our history are unfortunately uncommon) the most prosperous cultures are inevitably those geared towards pacifistic endeavors; developments of technology for the common good, of elaborate education and social engineering on a grand scale. When peace ends, these cultures suffer; much like France suffered in the world wars, and Poland too, today we view the world and see that in our brief period of peace (at least outside of the undeveloped world) some of the greater advances man has made have come from hedonistic and pacifistic states like Sweden and, strangely, Germany- but now these states are devouring the wrong food in the wrong quantities- no longer do they even seek to preserve their cultures, because they have become convinced that their cultures are largely not worth saving. Sadly, the cultures most given to this willful suicidal tendency are generally the least deserving of destruction, at least if we apply a subjective morality that includes applause for not slaughtering people in other lands, and focusing instead on improving the human condition through arts and education and literature and philosophy, and a live-and-let-live ethos of quasi-pacifism that sets them apart from nations still using a full military industrial complex.

A civic or cultural nationalist then cannot be against immigration but they have to comprehend, if intelligent, that not all cultures are the same, and thus are not equal on a social, technological, or academic basis. Their values are not the same.

IMPROVING THE STATE

A person raised in a destabilized third world state in which a junta or mob largely runs roughshod over whatever weak government exists there will have a vastly different understanding of the world from someone raised in the comfort of a fully stable nation with values borne not out of struggle but an age of the lack thereof. If we consider the Western European of today, they appear to be primarily motivated in their voting habits and activism by a desire to avoid all conflict, and simply ingratiate themselves economically by making themselves more and more privy to social spending and niche programs often designed by an interventionist-derived system of bureaucrats which decrease its efficiency. If we look instead at cultures which are wracked by violence, famine, disease, or lack of technological advancement, and continue in what amounts to tenant farming and survivalism with a state that has no significance outside of its capitol or perhaps a few larger metropolitan areas (we might think of the Sudan, or perhaps Sierra Leone or something of that nature) the population there is being developed and raised generation after generation with nothing on their mind but surviving, and if lucky, if very skilled, perhaps leaving altogether to go find glorious peaceful reprieve and wealth in the western world, where they will inevitably find that their drive and ambition are major assets, because the people they are now competing with for employment, academic advancement, or anything else, have not been raised to fight and struggle, and have become, over time, weak and less able to compete with these foreigners. This in turn causes two problems.

First, the native country, the less developed state, is given brain drain because its top students and entrepreneurs have left altogether.

Second, the host nation has increase in social alienation because the native culture feels threatened by the foreigner even if the foreigner is lawful and hard working. Arguably, the opposite is even worse; that immigrants have arrived and show no aptitude and are merely fleeing destabilization and have a misconception that western states and bureaucrats actually exist to help them and have the ability to do so. If a hedonistic western population adopts a handful of refugees this is probably true; it matters little to anyone because the cost is slight and they can claim it as a moral virtue. Then, though, once that first wave of newcomers is fed, sheltered, and given jobs, more will generally come to take advantage of this option handed to them by these rich, pacifistic first worlders. Unfortunately, at some point, public opinion begins to grow more and more nativistic or populism takes hold, and the foreigners are mistreated or expelled altogether.

We cannot blame the native or the foreigner for this shift. The foreigner wants nothing more than basic dignity- so too does the native- but the state has become imbalanced due to the negligence of the state itself, the government and bureaucrats eventually forsake common sense and admit anyone regardless of their qualities- up to and including overrunning its own nation with millions of outsiders who show little proclivity towards any form of assimilation. When these foreigners inevitably adopt criminal tendencies because there are no longer enough jobs for them, and because the budget for handouts cannot increase eternally, the foreigner becomes a criminal and the hardened nativist is now able to convince, over time, even the most hedonistic and pacifistic leftist elements that he was "right all along." The left thus washes the hand of the right and exonerates it of potential eventual violence, because it has enabled its arguments, just as the right, when it over-stretches its traditionalism in due time, exonerates the left and gives it the excuse for revolutionary habits because it has fulfilled the arguments of the left. Both sides destabilize a state and ought to be avoided vigorously.

III: Resolved; that the Primitive Ancestors of All Social Systems other than Communalism are Present in Archaeology

We may say that of all of the cultural life forms present today or in recent history in the world are present and evident to a degree within archaeology- from the archaic period through antiquity- with the sole exception of communal authoritarianism, better known by its proponents variously as Marxism, Communism, or in its slow, creeping, chronic form, "Socialism."

When we observe the megaliths of old we certainly see the primordial ancestor from which theocracy would eventually emerge on full display- we need look no further than the centrality and size of religious structures (or pre-religious as it may be) built by almost every substantially organized culture. "How" asks the modern man "did supposedly nomadic people, not significantly advanced beyond the hunter-gatherer stage, and using stone or at best copper tools, build, for example, Gobekli Tepe, and why?" The ruins there are vast- they have not even been fully excavated at this time. When Marx pledged himself to writing what would replace the Catholic Bible as the most butcherous work ever penned by man, and live to see the rudimentary beginning of various stages of genocide which would follow (which he probably observed with glee, since the first to die were the much hated bourgeois, those unfortunate enough to have garnered some degree of wealth in nations fallen to his warped world view) he was unfortunately not privy to modern anthropological theory and practice- had he waited, or been born later, he would have lived to see the foundation of his entire philosophy- primitive communism- utterly debased.

From the great megaliths of Rome to the Egyptian

pyramids, of mud brick or stone, and from the great halls of Petra, to the temples of early Hinduism, to well beyond, the centrality of spiritual structures of various sorts especially with regards to astrological lore and death and burial, reigns supreme through most early human history. When we observe that neanderthals buried belongings with the dead, without apparently (we suppose) having the concept of an afterlife, two interjections may be made to explain this phenomenon; first, what if they had a belief in this after all, and developed spirituality long before even a megalith had been built? Then they were sophisticated in the spiritual sense, perhaps they too had temples, and the remains are gone because they were made entirely of organic materials. Second, if they did not, then they apparently had a sense of belonging- of ownership. If we combine this with their evident tribalism, anything but communalism is evident.

We see also the rudimentary beginnings of nationalism, democracy, and oligarchy, along with the big man precursor to dictatorship in early man; all of these tendencies, created early and often, can be said to be innate to man; they were not the result of substantial theory, of great halls of scholars debating, they were natural inclinations developed before even writing existed, and before language was sophisticated. They were, amusingly, chosen in a quasi-communal sense! For these primitive people so-called were not deliberately so much as naturally ordering their societies; and they chose to include everything but the kitchen sink in their order, and everything except for communism.

The only instances of communal ownership that we see present were in societies in which statehood itself did not develop- these systems appear to invariably share two facets antithetical to Marxist philosophy; first, being tribal and family-based, and second being reciprocal and ordered. There is no element of anarchism present, so much as a very stringent order

evolving. And everything which emerges as an extension of his mind, his intellectual faculties, that is, must also evolve over time in accordance with similar principles.

This helpfully explains, without any real observation of subjective morality (sometimes claimed as objective outside of the realm of any objective reason why) the state of the world and of technology, the state of states themselves, the mannerisms of society and their meanderings, their change over time, and why some systems appear to never work.

Proponents of virtually every ideology proclaim that theirs is some 'highest' ideology which exceeds all others, giving a few reasons why. The monarchist proclaims that the benevolence of an unrestricted central order creates maximized efficiency. The communist proclaims that humans have been practically waiting for tens of thousands of years to inevitably evolve past the need for statehood altogether to live communally. The constitutional democrat or advocate of classical liberalism proclaims that all human order was in error for most of its existence and that a constrained representative system allows efficiency within liberty. The modern oligarchist tends to be a technocrat or advocates a strict meritocracy (which might be labeled as an aristocracy based on intellect rather than property or lineage) and proclaims that combining human order backwards with its own technological merits can literally save mankind. The dictator naturally sees him or herself as the arbiter of all proper order (we might think of modern day Turkmenistan here.) These are just a few ideologies.

How then do we determine which of these claims are 'right'? There is no solid objective basis upon which to do so for two reasons; first, that situations change and a system which maximizes its survivability in one era may be utterly debased in another. Second, morality must be, at least for the purposes of installing order, rendered secondary and considered as subjective, because so many opinions are claimed objective by their proponents, often to the mutual exclusion of one anothers' claims- to render any of these claims objective is to immediately destroy our own reasoning with bias. When I arrive at my conclusions here it will not be from any moral argument, but a biological and pragmatic one that happens to generally predispose me to support one system over all others, with a few tangential systems at least tolerable in nature to the exclusion of most others.

I propose simply a biological alternative to morals or other subjective arguments; which system most closely mimicks biology, and does this system appear capable of working, either as-is or as-was or in some potential modified form? From this I have explored different systems of governance, statehood, and so forth, and come to my biological conclusion.

I propose the general (not complete) superiority of constitutional governance; in which the state is constrained, given roles it is able to fill to the exclusion of all others, in which the population acknowledges and is enabled to defend its rights, and in which rights are enumerated (not given) in a form which is potentially malleable but extremely difficult to alter, such that it may only be modified and then probably only temporarily in time of extreme need.

The constitutional system is indeed the sort of missing link between anarchism (which devolves into mob rule almost invariably) and any authoritarian system (which often undergoes a revolution, leading to an alternative authoritarian variant, or which, due to lack of change on behalf of its leader or leaders, experiences detriment in some eras, and prosperity only in some.)

IMPROVING THE STATE

The proponents of authoritarianism say the government is a brain which commands the body, or population at whole. They make a biological argument here that is utterly wrong; yes, the brain commands movement, it tells the heart to beat and the limbs to coordinate, and if absent the life form dies (roughly akin to a stateless society, such as is envisioned by communists and anarchists) however, does the body not give feedback as well to the brain? The brain does not operate in a vacuum and, if it is deaf to the pains or desires of the body, the body will die as surely as if it did not have a brain at all. Government which is unconstrained appears to function more like a brain riddled with tumors in which more and more nutrition is commanded in order to endlessly replicate faulty cells (perhaps akin to ever growing bureaucracy and increasingly tyrannical semi-restrained systems which break their normal boundaries.) When I argue here for a constitutional system I do not argue for the systems used by modern republics; every one of them, to my knowledge, is stricken with cancer, otherwise known as bureaucracy beyond its proper order.

When cancer takes hold it is because of a faulty cellular function in which the literal biological constraints put upon cells-genetically, to prevent improper replication, are removed; this leads to endless out of control growth and mitosis, and strangulates the body. Untreated, it will almost surely kill the life form suffering from this abomination of genetics. Likewise, a state which suffers from prolonged bureaucratic growth, or prolonged growth of central government, will eventually die. For nations, death does not necessarily mean wholesale loss of life or conquering by a foreign state, it can also entail a revolution which resets its biology- states are able to reincarnate without losing their biological function, a strange statement potentially deserving of spiritual study by those who wish to ruminate upon its meaning, if cultural and political extensions from evolution are to be taken as a token and given import.

IMPROVING THE STATE

The constitution, properly understood and guarded, properly used, is like the strictures placed by the body upon its own cells in order to preserve their function.

A state requires not only a written constitution (preferably one not easily altered and in which it is easier to add more constraints than to remove them) but a population well ordered and intelligent enough to be armed and able to defend the same. Most forms of governance which have ever existed have died because government was too central and powerful not because its power was lacking or because the state was subjugated- especially in the modern era where the arms race itself has created a sort of regulatory system preventing outright conquest of land in most instances; this delicate order is almost certain to lead to the destruction of human order in due time, but that is a subject for a future chapter here.

If the population lacks a constitutional system the government may grow at a whim, and inevitably will in accordance with its biological tendencies- because it will be enabled to compete with the private market it will, more and more, amalgamate a core of wealth and power and become tyrannical and eventually break down altogether as it oversteps the tolerance of its subjects (for citizens do not exist unless they both have and preserve their rights, whether they are considered natural rights enumerated, or given rights guaranteed on paper in such a system.) If the population is unwilling or unable to defend such a system, the constitution thus in place lacks all purpose and will slowly be eroded according to the slow denigration that results from successive generations tolerating the degradation of their rights- we see this in its middle stages already in the United States, the beacon of the world which once so fervently protested even the slightest government imposture. Hopefully this trend will be reversed quickly, or we will fall into darkness.

V: The United States as Potentially Able to be Perfected

The United States, in its founding, was an essentially perfect base system that failed to be perfected because of perceived malleability in its constitution that was never meant to exist, and because of successive generations of Americans doing exactly what their intellectual founders suggested they not do; namely, sacrificing liberty for security- that they were lied to by the dishonest and told it was 'necessary' or that the loss of liberty was 'temporary' and would be reversed when time of danger ended is clear here; both were lies, both are lies, and will always be lies. One can be sure, when government proposes necessity it is almost always not, and when it claims its growth is temporary it will never be so. Gun control, touted as 'necessary' to defeat mobsters, was never actually necessary- ending prohibition (itself a tyrannical move when implemented) would have done far better. Raising taxes to pay for infrastructure that had already begun to sprawl across the continent was never necessary either and the fruits of this wanton spending are now evident; overgrowth and the dilapidation of older roads and highways that sit neglected as bureaucracy strangulates efficiency and prevents them from ever being properly cared for outside of regions where the population is exploding. Censorship on the radio and television has rendered those platforms, which ought by rights to be free, to virtual uselessness and the government will now proceed to constantly try to do the same to the internet (thankfully it is unlikely they will prevail- because it is far larger and more decentralized, and it isn't clear people will ever tolerate their attempts to any great degree.)

The essential model though of the United States' founding is generally perfect; the concept of checks and balances introduced, had they existed under a more constraining constitution, would probably be in properly regulated and working order even now had it not been for three unfortunate advents; judicial activism, executive overreach, and the partisanship which has strangled the legislature and prevented it from activating its own powers to suppress the other two parts of government which have become too powerful; and through this choking off of the legislature (which should never have become a partisan body to begin with) it has actually given up, it seems, its right to determine the constitution via amendment, ceding it generally to the supreme court and its subjugated federal courts, and to the presidency, which can now wage war without declaring it, as is the sole responsibility of the legislature. Generally the only limit experienced now by the executive branch, beyond the party of the 'foes' of the president stonewalling a few bills now and then introduced by the rest of the legislature, is itself judicial and takes the form of courts harassing the presidency regarding executive orders, sometimes fairly, often unfairly.

The partitioning of government is roughly akin to the proper function of a biological organism as well; the human brain, the rough equivalent of a governing body, is not monolithic, but contains several 'levels' of a sort, from the brain stem in its dumb, plodding monotony to the outer cortex in which higher thought functions are produced. The baser parts of the brain are related only to automatic bodily functions, and the lizard brain of sorts would tell the human to merely seek food, shelter, and mating, irrespective of higher thought, were the cortex not functioning and drawing on memory and learning to govern its actions further. Within a split government, with our three branches, each branch is properly understood to be meant to regulate the others, primarily to constrain the power of each branch as the other two overcome its attempts to break through regulation and become tyrannical.

IMPROVING THE STATE

The constitution itself though does not suffer from being difficult to understand so much as it suffers from being interpreted through successive generations by the corrupted concept that it was meant to be interpreted at all; it is not- it was meant to be malleable only with difficulty, and perhaps here is the seed which will send forth its vine to eventually kill off our tree of liberty, so to speak. We can use examples here.

The second amendment of the constitution explicitly protects specifically civilian firearm ownership, as well as the right of citizens to amalgamate into a standing militia in time of need to do so. The term "well regulated" in the mid 1700s did not mean regulated by legalism, or a government, but rather simple that something was performing properly; the well regulated militia thus must be properly armed and trained and capable of defending the nation against enemies foreign or domestic- it has little to do with hunting or sports shooting or gun collecting as some well meaning but utterly incorrect pro-gun advocates have tried to state.

But what is the militia? Some people think it again means something it does not; the militia, in modern terminology, is typically a quasi-civilian group armed with various weaponry, often with a penchant for being called dangerous or violent by mainstream culture. Many advocates of disarmament take it to mean the military, as in, the various soldiers fielded by the US government in an official capacity.

The term "militia" in the mid 18th century had nothing to do with a military order- indeed quite the opposite- the term "regulars" was generally used for the latter. A militia was a civilian force able to muster arms. In our case, any person capable of fighting, who is not a lunatic, a small child, or completely geriatric and bodily unsound. "Militia" is used specifically to differentiate the force spoken of in the second amendment from the very same standing army that some suggest it references!

The inter-state commerce clause might be seen though as the worst of all mistakes made in our founding, albeit the effects were suppressed until Franklin Roosevelt (the badly overrated socialist stooge who prolonged the depression and is remembered as a hero for having had polio) in 1937 successfully packed the supreme court with his socialistic cronies and began re-interpreting the constitution at a whim, invalidating even very recent decisions to preserve his "New Deal" (raw deal, for the working class population.)

But the constitution thankfully has one saving grace for our nation to restore the natural biological balance which should be the centerpiece of such a system; it can be expanded with amendments- a simple amendment re-defining the interstate commerce clause in its originally held narrow definition, and a second amendment explicitly naming the people at large as the receptacles of most of the other amendments (example; the second amendment, which does not pertain to an army, but rather to the entire population) would suffice fairly well and greatly prolong our existence as a free nation. A third could in fact be crafted to correct our problems with just as great of effect- an amendment to prevent bureaus, unions, corporate entities, foreign entities of any kind, lobbies, and other groups from participating in election fundraising, guaranteeing a one-person-one-donation system which will force politicians to appeal to their constituents instead of some business heads and bankers to bankroll them. Since we are a representative democracy it is sensible to suggest that this, which closely approaches actual democracy, would be in play, in the electoral sense, if nowhere else.

VI: The Population's Relative Powers and Weaknesses

The people of the United States barely even comprehend their own power over government and many are completely bitter and do not even vote, let alone do anything else. One can hardly blame the bitter because of the stagnation of our legislature and the seeming autocratic actions of the courts and presidency in the modern age. Many times when one beholds a debate on politics we see the politically active ridicule those who are less so, without realizing the central reason why they feel inactivity is the best solution to their problems.

The populations' power essentially takes the following forms:

First, a literate population is capable of arguing against abuse, to greater effect than a government is often capable of defending its own corruption.

Second, an armed population is capable of withstanding abuse through the threat of or use of force.

Third, a population with any semblance of significant private wealth can potentially strangulate its own economic system to purge the corrupt, forcing them out by using their wealth as a leverage against the productive system itself, forcing it to obey their demands (think here of a nationwide strike, or a large scale walk off and protest.)

Fourth, a population with a civic system held domestically in high regard (and preferably held in esteem by foreign peoples) can ideologically grandstand against their own government if the need arises, and assert their superiority over it with moral threat alone (importantly this is an emotional appeal of sorts, not objective, and acts upon the psyche of ones' fellow citizens.)

As such under these four powers we see four things that must be promulgated and defended for a people to remain free for any great length of time. The population must be armed, guaranteed academic and expressive liberty, literate enough to make use of the same powers, and contain in its essence a cultural pride able to withstand denigration by guilt tripping authoritarians which seek ever to use their own corrupted moral arguments to gain more power.

When we compare this to the modern state of most of the world these protections are invariably lacking in part and sometimes wholesale.

Many populations are disarmed in part or whole. Most of the world is not highly literate and even in literate nations much of the population does not understand philosophy or civics. Nations are often either too miserable to be in esteem or have developed a guilt complex through the corruption of globalists and social marxism. Most of the world is impoverished and in nations where abject poverty is less common the lower classes at best have enough to eat and not the liberty to walk off the job for days at a time to pressure their governments.

Safeguarding three of these things is easy; a simple constitutional provision can protect firearms and once obtained and retained they in turn can help protect everything else. Private wealth is generated by a largely free market environment, and thus reducing or eliminating interventionism while preventing monopolization is key. Civic pride can be organically generated. Literacy is generated by the will of the population and its ability to educate itself and alone is perhaps the hardest to obtain; how can one compel another to become intelligent? How can one coerce them to care enough to build literacy? Indeed, often, people feel they do not have the time to do so because the globalists have reduced them to little more than wage slave serfs through corporatism (which I will excoriate later) and this is centrally their greatest form of control and authoritarianism above anything else. Legislation meant to disarm the civilian population has never had so much of an effect as this worst of strategies. It declines literacy, reduces economic freedom, encourages authoritarianism in general, and even prevents many from affording a firearm. It is the worst of all evils.

All is hardly lost though, much of the world retains the kernel of pride even when fooled by those who tell them to feel guilty, and in the era of worldwide discourse it is possible for different nations to act in another biological manner; the exchange of information in almost a genetic sense. A proud but impoverished culture may impart pride to a rich but guilt tripped culture while the later imparts economic views organically which can partially solve poverty. Both organisms, both states, are greatly helped by this exchange- for this reason even more centrally than pride, firearms, or literacy, defense of electronic communication in as uncensored and raw a form as possible ought to be among the highest priorities of any liberty loving people. It is the greatest potential force for political and social good that has ever existed on our planet, and should be fiercely defended.

VII: Motivations for A System

We must examine what primordial mechanisms may be used to explain the rise of a state or quasi state, or any system as it is adhered to even outside a state, forming a core of power regardless, through guerrilla warfare or something similar, before any deeper reading into the stability of such systems may be made. In fact, their stability is also malleable and situational- although a fairly good general idea of its long term chance of stability and sovereignty is possible to get. When observing this we can ask "what is natural?" or rather, "what appears to show itself to be like unto natural because it is able to be implemented, is effective, and is stable?"

First then we see states and groups crafted primarily out of malice. When Che Guevara was attempting to undermine various governments and economic systems this appears to have indeed been on his mind. This figure, applauded invariably by those who do not understand his life or opinions, spoke ill in a manner not unlike Pol Pot about many of those around him and pledged himself to slaughtering people who often were just civilians who were too wealthy for his own taste (this did not stop him from obtaining and using his own luxury goods.) A group which seeks power may exist solely, thus, for the benefit of a lunatic or tyrant- and while we often tell tales of some rogue or miscreant gathering an army to try and usurp the throne in some fantastic tale of the middle ages, it is more common that rogues and miscreants rise out of less corrupted systems by destroying them from the inside. States seldom die off from external forces, corruption rarely begins through exterior subversion, it begins internally, albeit sometimes prodded on by an exterior force.

We see also groups which have, seek to have, or seek to

continue having, power, out of 'necessity.' The modern United States is more and more an example of this sad state in which a massive complex formed between career politicians, the corporate media, and international banks attempts to fool people into thinking they are under attack so that it can justify attacking other people outside of the United States or, perhaps even more worryingly, to suppress internal groups or opinions they deem harmful. It is important to remember that when a government stresses that something is necessary, it is almost always not necessary, and is usually at best one of a number of solutions-often, it's the outright worst thing one can do under a situation they themselves often manufactured to begin with.

The modern United States in its order through necessity stands almost diametrically opposed to its founding system; revolutionary thought was a motivation from the desire for the most basic and constrained of orders, with the notion that a small, constrained order was more stable, and that a population could largely manage its own affairs. Of all forms of order the revolutionary type, which seeks to limit the very system it creates, using a constitution or other means, is unique, and possibly the only one which (properly engineered) is capable of lasting for any great degree of time. The aforementioned ability to expand the constraint placed upon government is the failsafe that we will hopefully use to restore our Republic before it withers and dies due to too much bureaucracy.

There are other, less important forms of order; blood lineage (monarchy) or appeals to intellectual superiority (meritocracy, which is just the mating of an oligarchy with the primitive big man system of pre-state era dictatorship.) These have largely died off and are more or less irrelevant. Sadly even a monarchy is capable (with a good monarch) of performing more efficiently and with less abuse than communalism or a system which uses 'necessity' to justify all poor acts.

VIII: The Necessity of Power and of Constraining it

As aforementioned any stable system must contain two seemingly paradoxical elements which war against one another; it must be able to change but it must be resistant to changing its core value system. At the same time it must be limited but efficient and able to respond to external perturbation from any exterior or subversive interior force. A state under anarchy will be unable to defend itself, a state under strangulation from too many laws, too many lawyers, too much bureaucracy, will eventually fall into the same trap. Linear scales are often far too simplistic to explain political or social systems (which are better arranged into a three dimensional matrix, overlapping with others, with great convolution and confusion over minutiae) but the scale of order itself may be rendered linear, or rather, a series of lines. The state is not the only arbiter of order in a constitutional society, the population at large and, separately, their private organizations and business entities both have their own gradients of order and disorder.

So on the one end, anarchism reigns; there is no order at all, everyone will do as they please, they are completely free- but their freedom is unstable, subjected to constant risk of mob rule or invasion, because no coherent organizational structure exists beyond the strictly voluntary to deal with either issue. Disasters cannot be easily recovered from. An epidemic would be utterly horrifying.

On the other end, the strangulated order begins to roughly resemble the other end of the pole. We might take this line and wrap it into a circle as people began doing with the interplay between communism and fascism after the second world war- the two systems, which claimed to be utterly opposite, when arranged on the basis of how abusive they were, began to merge together, with the other 'side' of the circle representing far greater liberty, if not actual anarchism. The end result of anarchism is the same as the end result of limitless authority- they both break down and destabilize, and are replaced by something else, which may indeed be even worse than the dying system of yesteryear.

Power corrupts; what then is needed is the limitation of any and all sources of power within a society. Government should compete with itself by being split into sections. Civilians should compete with the government by having their own specific powers to themselves. Government should instill order as well on the population when needed, while being constrained as to the scope of its size and power. Here is something few notice; the government constrains the power of the individual, in order to craft balance the individual must be similarly capable of constraining government power. Any other system cannot contain balance. This is the bane of all non-constitutional systems, especially those lacking an armed and aware population. This is also why any sane economic system must be predominantly a free market with capitalism- businesses compete with one another, increasing wages, decreasing prices, and generally maintaining efficiency because they compete. I will say here (and echo this in a section later against corporatism at length) that the only significant interventionism that government ought to be allowed is an ability to destroy monopolies and trusts to re-inject efficient competition back into a free market that it otherwise leaves to its own devices. Again, balance must of necessity exist, otherwise at least one source of power lacks, and suffers as the result. Today, in the United States, it is the civilian population suffering the most, along with any and all smaller, non-corporate entities they spawn in a market that is at most half free.

IX: States Have Generally Improved Until Recently

The natural order of evolution on a cultural basis, towards ever more stable forms of governance, has been continuous until fairly recently in man's history. Up until the interwar period, the general trend was towards freedom and liberty and away from tyranny, culminating in the first wave of globalism, which was actually a positive one; we have to be honest here, globalism was originally dreamed up by well meaning idealists as a way to prevent war and create harmony. Unfortunately, it was quickly understood by the corrupt as an excellent vessel for their greed and avarice, and soon darker minds seized control of the early globalist structures once created, as a means to perpetuate their industrial income, their stranglehold on all populations, and their proxy wars once they realized that constant low, simmering fighting was more profitable than outright conquest.

Indeed, the move from imperialism to globalism and proxy conflict was less about reducing human misery than a move to improve the image of the same people responsible for misery and warfare. The globalists were worried that any imperial regime they backed would eventually shun and destroy them and consolidate a new world order under their own dictatorial system, destroying its own original funding apparatus. What better way to control the world than to preserve the illusion of conflict between states led by people who indeed are very much alike? It is far easier; the same multinational banks and corporate entities produce weapons for both sides of any limited, controlled conflict, usually using the corporate media to excuse themselves as liberators. This is a fairly modern development replacing imperialism in the generally European sense, and nationalism the world over.

Nationalism is superior insofar as it is not led by imperialists- far superior to globalism. The modern day self proclaimed messiahs of social justice and of peace have the right idea but fail to identify the same governing bodies and their auxiliary corporate backers as the actual cause of the disease they have identified- nationalism itself is not responsible and is merely a cultural or ethnic reflection irrespective of whatever economic or social policy is implemented. Until the last century, every culture was nationalistic, including those which were ultimately little removed from outright pacifism and were too busy studying academics to care much for waging war.

Liberty can never be perpetuated so long as the corporate and banking apparatus remains intact. The apparatus contains most of the wealth of the world, regardless of the economic policies used by states it involves. The few states outside of this apparatus are little more than pawns of those that are, and which benefit from a large military presence; the world in 1900 was primarily ruled by a half dozen major powers; the United States, the British Empire, the French, the Germans, the Russians... In 1950 The United States and Soviet Union had consolidated most of the world under their thumbs. The Non Aligned nations were never non aligned in anything but name- now China and the upstart European Union (which is dying anyways) share some of this monumental power- but all of these groups are fundamentally controlled by the same entities. About the only thing globalism never accounted for was the risk of nuclear war because their ability to control nuclear states is more limited if some upstart populist manages to grab power using their own corrupt methods. Some fear the current president of the United States (Donald Trump) is such a character- which could be the case, and could result in either great good or great evil.

X: Against Corporatism, the Worst Evil in Our Nation Today

It is now quite common for people to blame capitalism in specific for most of the problems present in the western world; these individuals conflate capitalism with corporatism and proclaim that the monster they observe is also fascism. At the same time, some confused moral conservatives proclaim it to be outright socialism. Pure confusion; so what monster exactly are we dealing with and how may it be done away with?

The answer is corporatism- this hideous being seems to spring up from out of any system it chooses to be birthed by- the Soviets were under a de facto corporatist system once the era of Stalin ended, when "reforms" were implemented, to take a fully centrally planned system and render it into a mixed model with interventionism; the authoritarianism remained as well, because corporatism does not care whether the population is specifically more or less socially free. The United States is dangerously close to operating under a corporatist economic model now as well, albeit the people here enjoy greater fiscal and social liberty than the Soviets ever did; perhaps the corporate and banker masters running this chimeric system realized that people had to be given the illusion of freedom and then be encouraged to spend themselves into debt as often as they can to keep the whole economy going when it's driven by monopolies which we once rightfully broke apart to encourage actual competition.

Merriam Webster gives us a perfectly fine definition of capitalism...

"an economic system characterized by private or corporate ownership of capital goods, by investments that are determined by private decision, and by prices, production, and the distribution of goods that are determined mainly by competition in a free market."

Do we operate under such a system? The government of the United States long ago introduced interventionist means to control prices, owns a large proportion of all the land in our nation, creates trade deals which inject external economic competition by states which manipulate their currency or their prices in general and which are sometimes centrally planned. Large corporate entities in the United States take advantage of a massive and convoluted tax code to pay very little while more productive and sometimes more intelligent small businesses and entrepreneurs get hammered by the actually large business tax rate. The government, at a seeming whim, can even ban the production, distribution, and use of some goods on a moral basis, even when there is no pragmatic reason to do so.

I say further that capitalism merely requires two things; maximized or nearly maximized competition in all areas of industry and commerce (including among the self employed) and a level playing field. It is perhaps important here to state that I am not suggesting we privatize "everything"- merely that where a private market exists (and it almost always, but not strictly always, should, for anything able to be profit-driven and productive and thus efficient) it should be largely left alone, and that business entities should not ever be given government grants, incentives, or favorable tax treatment for any reason. Because none of this is the case, we do not operate under capitalism, and corporate interventionism as we may term our actual operative economic and social strategy, is as far from capitalism as quasi-socialism or even fascism-lite. Indeed, the same people worried right now about fascism have been largely living under it for half a century; and it was mostly because of the same "Leftist" parties they applaud that we devolved to that degree away from a truly free market with actual competition.

The government does not need to directly attack a business firm or industry, by the way, to denigrate it; it simply funds and treats favorably its competitors. I have used the analogy of a simplified store which only sells two things; two virtually identical brands of bread. In order to denigrate one of these bread making firms, the business merely has to advertise or subsidize its competitor. The governments of the west do this every single day. Is this capitalism?

The solution is extremely simple; corporatism is in essence very vulnerable towards being torn apart so actual capitalism can reign again. I speak not of the draconian "privatize everything" methodology of anarchocapitalism; it is perfectly acceptable for a few critical types of work to be government co-opted (preferably at the state, not federal level, as I believe we ought to do with our educational system; it was far more effective when the states almost completely ran it!)

The solution is a vastly simplified tax code; drop the business tax rate and do away with write-offs and subsidies altogether so that the mom and pop store can compete with the multinational firm. Rip apart trade deals and any of their content that interferes with private economic systems. Dedicate government not to helping industry at the highest rung but balancing it to rip apart aging and inefficient monopolies; this sounds like an early 1900s progressivist tract, but the progressives never simplified the tax code and never did what I suggest to finalize the move back to capitalism; remove all reason for corporations to interfere with government by passing a constitutional amendment to limit election funding to one-person-one-donation and one-business-one-donation and cap both of these to keep big money out of the political arena to a great extent. Removing business altogether from electioneering seems like a bad idea, to me; businesses I feel, their ownership rather, has a ball in the game of what our nation decides to do, but their influence is far too great and should be vastly more limited; likewise, not a cent should ever be donated by any firm with foreign branches or which is not completely owned within the United States. Any business seeking to donate to or campaign on behalf of a political figure or party ought not to so much as have its mailbox in Jamaica for tax purposes.

Indeed it must sound strange, a capitalist proclaiming that corporations have no significant place in politics and are often intolerably inefficient! It sounds strange because many have been misled into believing that business is best managed by a handful of massive industrial and commercial firms and banks, when the true life blood of capitalism is your local or regional chain or mom and pop store, or the college aged group of entrepreneurs in their garage attempting to compile a computer program that they know can make them wealthier. This is the free market, this is competition- not favoritism shown towards business entities which merely happen to fund a political campaign. There shouldn't even bee PACs and super PACs, lobbies and bureaus and unions should not be donating to anyone. It's as simplistic as starving the government of any state of such donations, after which they are forced to represent the population as a whole and, second to this, business as a whole, including the smaller firms and upstarts they currently ignore. Only once we do this (and the sooner the better) will we be capitalists and will our nation improve fiscally and socially. Moral issues will decline in popularity as election material as well, since a wealthier population is typically under less stress.

XI: A Nation Must Preserve Identity

We now turn to another situation in which I must differ from the average libertarian or anarchocapitalist, while agreeing with them both in spirit on many issues. Here, though, I agree with nationalists, both civic and ethnic (for they lead to similar end results despite the griping of both groups.) The core essence, the spirit, of a nation, must be vigorously preserved. To each people, again whether based on the ethnic model (as most of the old world) or a civic one (as most of the new world states) there is a right to determine what they do and do not wish to do, and what form they wish their society, including the state, to take. It is as dangerous to them that their cultural values should shift (internally or as the result of external pressure) as that their economic model should be overthrown.

Each people should consider themselves as superior regardless of their values; there is no objective "our people/race/nation is better than everyone else" but it should be the operative assumption regardless, because it helps to keep the nation stable. Likewise, a people must be willing to defend those values and their freedom, up to and including being willing to cast the evil eye on those who pretend to be helping to defend their values when in reality they do not. I recall that during the early days of the invasion of Iraq by the US and our so called coalition of nations, that the government and its corporate and fiscal backers were more than willing to cast the entire situation as a struggle for liberation and berate its critics as unpatriotic; most people swallowed the bait and thus allowed our government to destabilize a state on false pretenses with no benefit and much detriment to the lives of thousands of our troops, and our economy as well at a massive level through enormous spending. It costs a lot of money to bomb people for no reason. Sadly, the arms industry (interventionism in its prime form) made a mint manufacturing weapons and vehicles while our people never saw a cent of productivity unless they were employed as government workers or private workers in a firm chosen to manufacture such things. In reality, the government itself, its decision, was unpatriotic and so were the firms making money off the disaster we had involved our country in. If only more people had resisted the buzz words in times of post-terroristic stress and bothered to question the motives of uncle sam in its actions, we'd be in a vastly different and probably far better world.

A people must be just as wary of its government acting badly as it ought to be of foreign states or groups attempting to interfere in its affairs. Such interference on either end is inevitably good for those corrupt folks interfering and inevitably at best neutral and usually bad for everyone else. Our founding ethos was liberty, not overthrowing random dictators and installing weak "democracies" so-called in order to continue making money for business firms which donated to the political party that happens to be in charge at the time.

This extends past any party; all large parties in the world appear to be compromised by the same figures and interventionist systems. It would be better if we had no political parties at all, but distrusting them and forcing them to prove their merit in each proposal they make is an acceptable proposition in place of a better way that was already dead two centuries ago as partisan electioneering developed in areas it was meant to be absent in.

XII: Conclusion

The process of improving and stabilizing a state through the alteration of its governing body is legally complicated but theoretically and fundamentally simple, requiring only the will to do so, at least, for an armed population which exists already under a constitutional system. Elsewhere, an uprising would need to first install a constitution and hope that it is well crafted.

At most the United States is fundamentally three constitutional amendments from long term stability- not so very much after all; one to suppress corporatism in a fiscal sense, one to properly modulate elections and their financing, and one to "expand" (rephrase) the first, second, and fourth amendments to make it clear that speech is free of censorship- including censorship laid down by government co-opting private orders, that the militia is the population and their right to bear any and all small arms is limitless and not situational or subject to fine or fee, and that the right to privacy extends to all electronic correspondence. It is additionally possible for a fourth new amendment to be crafted in order to suppress excessive taxation and fees by permanently putting a cap on the percentage of productivity which may ever be taxed or population which the government may ever employ at one time, twain with a permanent cap on the income of such bureaucrats.

I then submit the final act which does not require, strictly, a constitutional amendment but a legislative move only, to craft a bill that automatically strikes down any law, penalty, licensing fee, or bureau's standing if not reauthorized on a four year basis.

It is my strongly held belief that regardless of a nation's general cultural value system or other composition, it is greatly helped and usually more efficient when personal freedom is maximized. True, we might occasionally catch ourselves wishing we had "a benevolent dictator" to "clean house and get rid of all the scumbags"- indeed, it would be nice if that could happen, but the power they would amalgamate would corrupt them in due time; far better for the constraint of government to expand enough so that corruption can never take hold- specifically because significant power over most affairs is never given to them.

If the government is to be seen as the brain of a nation (often a deficient one!) then we ought to keep its thinking on the right subjects and teach it not to wander so much, lest it trip up and fall and bruise our society. I believe that perhaps we should see the people as the brain though and the government as little more than just the brain stem, required for a few rudimentary and near-automated functions such as maintaining a naval force and levying a limited, reasonable taxation for the purpose of funding the most critical of infrastructure (more important now in a fully industrial era than it was in the late 1700s, I admit.)

I realize of course that the main stumbling block to liberty is a government that has already violated most of the rights of the citizenry and reacts with great anger towards those that suggest it be more limited, and which constantly tries to cause its own citizens (an act akin in my mind to treason) to bicker and fight over issues which have little relevance. A severely constrained government can never be abusive whether it is run by the so-called right or so-called left. It lacks the power to be abusive. Nobody gains anything by empowering a government to greater degrees except in times of literal and abject disaster.

THE END